The Complete Guitar Player Songbook No. 2

by Russ Shipton

29	All My Trials	32	Mr Bojangles
3	America	26	Only Hopes Returning
24	April Come She Will	34	Plumstones
4	Bill Bailey	21	Ridin' Blind
20	The Black Velvet Band	14	San Francisco Bay Blues
13	Both Sides Now	44	Skyline
36	The Boxer	14	Slip Slidin' Away
24	Carolina In My Mind	25	The Sloop John B.
48	Classical Capers	45	Snowmobiling
30	Diamonds And Rust	39	Something
37	Early Mornin' Rain	18	Sundown
38	Fire And Rain	42	Sunny Afternoon
28	Frankie And Johnny	10	Sweet Baby James
5	Guantanamera	19	Take It Easy
46	G. Wizz	35	There But For Fortune
27	Help	46	The Third Waltz
43	Here Comes The Sun	9	The Universal Soldier
8	Homeward Bound	11	The Waltz Of Love
33	I'll Have To Say I Love You In A Song	4	Whiskey In The Jar
22	Imagine	12	The Wild Rover
40	Just The Way You Are	7	Wild World
23	Kumbaya	28	Worried Man Blues
16	Lyin' Eyes	6	The Wreck Of The Edmund Fitzgerald
41	May You Never	31	Your Song
17	Money's The Word	47	You've Got A Friend

Amsco Publications
London/New York/Sydney/Cologne

Amsco Publications
New York/London/Sydney

Music Sales Corporation
257 Park Avenue South, New York, NY 10010 USA

Music Sales Limited
8/9 Frith Street, London W1V 5TZ England

Music Sales Pty. Limited
120 Rothschild Street, Rosebery, Sydney, NSW 2018, Australia

This book Copyright © 1982 by Wise Publications.
Published 1984 by Amsco Publications,
A Division of Music Sales Corporation, New York, NY.

Order No. AM 31634
International Standard Book Number: 0.8256.2328.6

All rights reserved. No part of this book may be
reproduced in any form or by any electronic or mechanical means
including information storage and retrieval systems,
without permission in writing from the publisher.

Art direction by Mike Bell
Cover illustration by Keith Richens

Printed in the United States of America by
Vicks Lithograph and Printing Corporation

Tablature sample (one bar)

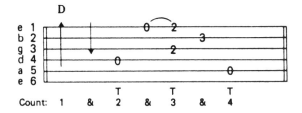

Notes:
a) D (indicated above tab.) = chord to be fingered.
b) ↑ = *down*ward strum.
c) ↓ = *up*ward strum.
d) Numbers on lines (strings) = open string or fret to be fingered and played.
e) 0̂ 2 = an open string hammered on to the 2nd fret.
f) T (indicated below tab.) = right hand thumb. For other notes, right hand fingers are used.
g) Where 'swing' is indicated before the song, the notes between beats are delayed.

America Paul Simon

3/4 Rhythm/Strumming.
See Course Book No. 1 Page 9.

"Kathy," I said, as we boarded a Greyhound in Pittsburgh
"Michigan seems like a dream to me now.
"It took me four days to hitchhike from Saginaw
"I've come to look for America."
Laughing on the bus, playing games with the faces
She said the man in the gaberdine suit was a spy
I said "Be careful, his bowtie is really a camera
Toss me a cigarette, I think there's one in my raincoat."
"We smoked the last one an hour ago."
So I looked at the scenery, she read her magazine
And the moon rose over an open field
"Kathy, I'm lost," I said, though I knew she was sleeping
"I'm empty and aching and I don't know why."
Counting the cars on the New Jersey Turnpike
They've all come to look for America
All come to look for America
All come to look for America.

© Copyright 1968 Paul Simon.
All Rights Reserved. International Copyright Secured.
Used by permission.

Bill Bailey — Traditional, arranged Russ Shipton

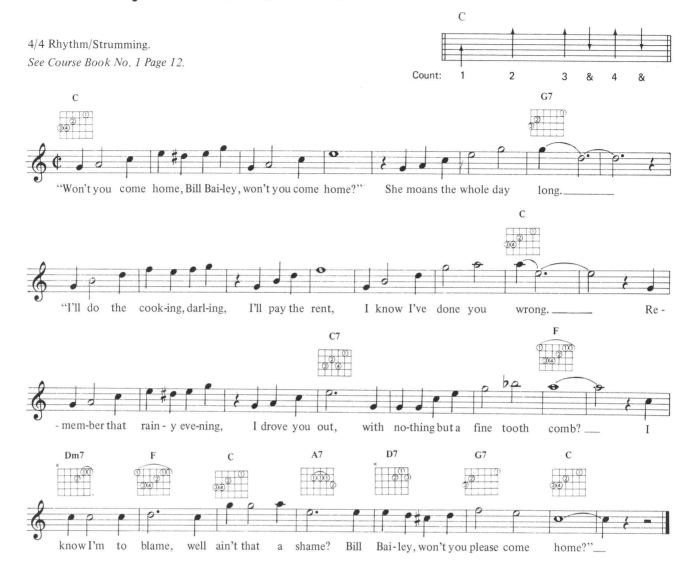

Whiskey In The Jar — Traditional, arranged Russ Shipton

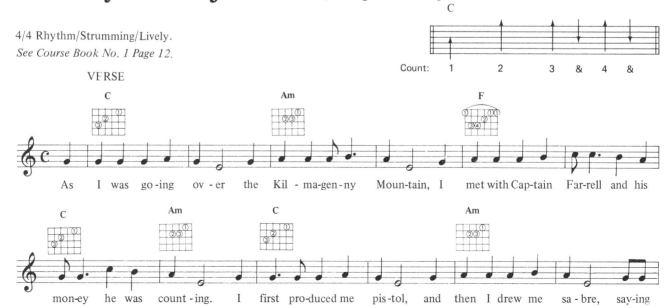

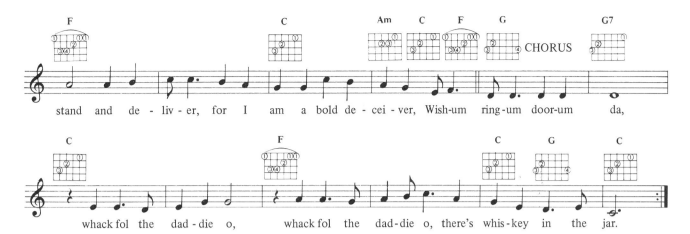

Verse 2:
He counted out his money, and it made a pretty penny
I put it in me pocket, and took it home to Jenny
She sighed and she swore that she never would betray me
But the devil take the women for they never can be easy.

Verse 3:
I went into me chamber, for to take a slumber
I dreamt of gold and jewels and for sure it was no wonder
For Jenny drew me charges, and she filled them up with water
And she sent for Captain Farrell to be ready for the slaughter.

Verse 4:
And it was early in the morning, before I rose to travel
Up comes a band of footmen and likewise Captain Farrell
I then produced me pistol, for she'd stole away me sabre
But I couldn't shoot the water, so a prisoner I was taken.

Verse 5:
Now if anyone can aid me, it's me brother in the army
If I could learn his station be it Cork or in Killarney
And if he'd come and join me, we'd go roving in Kilkenny
I'll engage he'd treat me fairer than me darling sporting Jenny.

Guantanamera
Words by Jose Marti. Music adaptation by Hector Angulo & Pete Seeger

4/4 Rhythm/Strumming.
See Course Book No. 1 Page 14.

Verse 2:
Mi verso es de un verde claro
Y de un carmin encendido
Mi verso es un cierro herido
Que busca en el monte amparo.

Verse 3:
Con los pobres de la tierra
Quiero yo mi suerte echar
El arroyo de la sierra
Me complace mas que el mar.

© Copyright 1963 and 1965 Fall River Music Inc.
All Rights Reserved. International Copyright Secured.

The Wreck Of The Edmund Fitzgerald

Gordon Lightfoot

3/4 Rhythm/Strumming.
See Course Book No. 1 Page 14.

1. The leg-end lives on from the Chip-pe-wa on down, of the big lake they call "Git-che Gu-mee."
2. The lake, it is said, nev-er gives up her dead, when the skies of No-vem-ber turn gloom-y.
3. With a load of iron ore twenty six thou-sand tons more than the Ed-mund Fitz-ge-rald weighed emp-ty,
4. That good ship and true was a bone to be chewed, when the gales of No-vem-ber came ear-ly.

Verse 2:

The ship was the pride of the American side
Coming back from some mill in Wisconsin.
As the big freighters go it was bigger than most
With a crew and good captain well-seasoned.
Concluding some terms with a couple of steel firms
When they left fully loaded for Cleveland.
And later that night when the ship's bell rang
Could it be the north wind they'd been feeling?

Verse 3:

The wind in the wires made a tattletale sound
And a wave broke over the railing
And every man knew as the captain did too
'Twas the witch of November come stealing.
The dawn came late and the breakfast had to wait
When the gales of November came slashing.
When afternoon came it was freezing rain
In the face of a hurricane west wind.

Verse 4:

When suppertime came the old cook came on deck saying:
"Fellas, it's too rough to feed you."
At seven p.m. a main hatchway caved in, he said:
"Fellas, it's been good to know you."
The captain wired in he had water coming in
And the good ship and crew was in peril.
And later that night when his lights went out of sight
Came the wreck of the Edmund Fitzgerald.

Verse 5:

Does anyone know where the love of God goes
When the waves turn the minutes to hours?
The searchers all say they'd have made Whitefish Bay
If they'd put fifteen more miles behind her.
They might have split up or they might have capsized
They may have broke deep and took water.
And all that remains is the faces and the names
Of the wives and the sons and the daughters.

Verse 6:

Lake Huron rolls, Superior swings in
In the rooms of her ice-water mansion.
Old Michigan steams like a young man's dreams
The island and bays are for sportsmen.
And farther below Lake Ontario
Takes in what Lake Erie can send her.
And the iron boats go as the mariners all know
With the gales of November remembered.

Verse 7:

In a musty old hall in Detroit they prayed
In the Maritime Sailors' Cathedral.
The church bell chimed till it rang twenty nine times
For each man on the Edmund Fitzgerald.
The legend lives on from the Chippewa on
Down of the big lake they called Gitche Gumee.
"Superior", they said, "never gives up her dead"
"When the gales of November come early."

© Copyright 1976 by Moose Music Ltd.
All Rights Reserved. Used by permission.

Wild World   Cat Stevens

4/4 Rhythm/Ballad strum.
See Course Book No. 1 Page 14.

Verse 2:
You know I've seen a lot of what the world can do
And it's breaking my heart in two
Because I never want to see you sad, girl
Don't be a bad girl
But if you wanna leave, take good care
Hope you make a lot of nice friends out there
But just remember there's a lot of bad air and beware.

© Copyright 1970 Freshwater Music Ltd., London, England.
All rights for the U.S.A. and Canada controlled by ACKEE MUSIC, INC.
International Copyright Secured. All Rights Reserved. Used by permission.

Book 1

Homeward Bound Paul Simon

4/4 Rhythm/Bass-strum.
See Course Book No. 1 Pages 14 & 22.

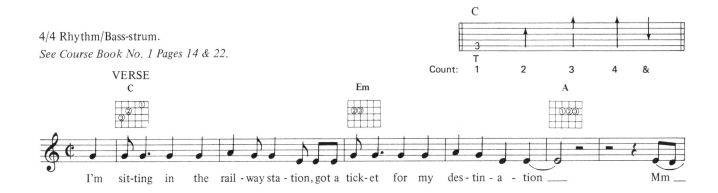

I'm sit-ting in the rail-way sta-tion, got a tick-et for my des-ti-na-tion___ Mm___

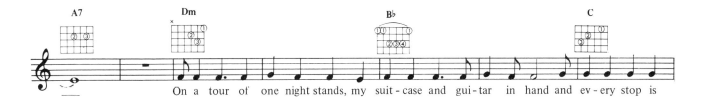

On a tour of one night stands, my suit-case and gui-tar in hand and ev-ery stop is

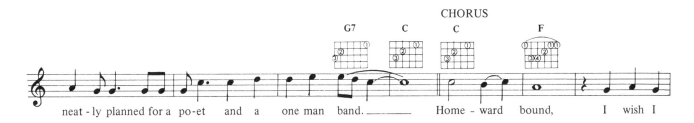

neat-ly planned for a po-et and a one man band.___ Home-ward bound, I wish I

was,___ home-ward___ bound. Home, where my thoughts es - ca-ping; home, where my

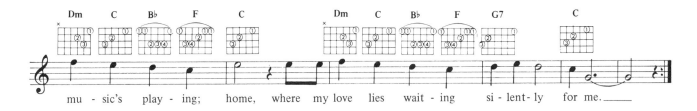

mu-sic's play-ing; home, where my love lies wait-ing si-lent-ly for me.___

Verse 2:

Every day's an endless stream
Of cigarettes and magazines
And each town looks the same to me
The movies and the factories
And every stranger's face I see
Reminds me that I long to be.

Verse 3:

Tonight I'll sing my songs again
I'll play the game and pretend
But all my words come back to me
In shades of mediocrity
Like emptiness in harmony
I need someone to comfort me.

© 1966 Paul Simon.
All Rights Reserved. International Copyright Secured. Used by permission.

The Universal Soldier — Buffy Sainte-Marie

4/4 Rhythm/Bass - strum.
See Course Book No. 1 Page 15.

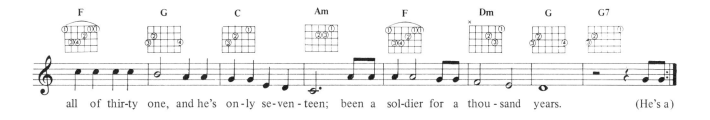

He's five foot two and he's six feet four; he fights with miss-iles and with spears; he's all of thir-ty one, and he's on-ly se-ven-teen; been a sol-dier for a thou-sand years. (He's a)

Verse 2:
He's a Catholic, a Hindu, an Atheist, a Jain
A Buddhist and a Baptist and a Jew
And he knows he shouldn't kill, and he knows he always will
Kill you for me, my friend, and me for you.

Verse 3:
And he's fighting for Canada, he's fighting for France
He's fighting for the U.S.A.
And he's fighting for the Russians and he's fighting for Japan
And he thinks we'll put an end to war this way.

Verse 4:
And he's fighting for democracy, he's fighting for the Reds
He says it's for the peace of all
He's the one who must decide who's to live and who's to die
And he never sees the writing on the wall.

Verse 5:
But without him how would Hitler have condemned him at Dachau?
Without him Caesar would have stood alone
He's the one who gives his body as a weapon of the war
And without him all this killing can't go on.

Verse 6:
He's the universal soldier, and he really is to blame
His orders come from far away no more
They come from here and there, and you and me
And Brothers, can't you see
This is not the way we put an end to war.

© Copyright 1963 by Woodmere Music.
All Rights Reserved. International Copyright Secured.

Sweet Baby James — James Taylor

3/4 Rhythm/Bass - strum.
See Course Book No. 1 Page 17.

Verse 2:
Now the first of December was covered in snow
And so was the turnpike from Stockbridge to Boston
The Berkshires seemed dreamlike on account of that frosting
With ten miles behind me and ten thousand more to go
There's a song that they sing when they take to the highway
A song that they sing when they take to the sea
A song that they sing of their home in the sky
Maybe you can believe it if it helps you to sleep
But singing works just fine for me.

Copyright © 1970 Blackwood Music Inc. and Country Road Music Inc.
administered by Blackwood Music Inc.
All Rights Reserved. International Copyright Secured. Used by permission.

The Waltz Of Love — Russ Shipton

3/4 Rhythm/Bass - strum.
See Course Book No. 1 Page 22.

Verse 2:
Out on the dance floor we smile and we stare
Our feet move with someone who cannot be there
While the band plays the old and familiar air
Let's dance to the waltz of love.

Verse 3:
Down off the clouds maybe crawl from the floor
Some fools protest yet they come back for more
They hear the band play "Love is life, so be sure —
You dance to the waltz of love".

© Copyright 1982 Dorsey Bros. Music, a division of Music Sales Corporation, New York, NY
All Rights Reserved. International Copyright Secured.

The Wild Rover
Traditional, arranged Russ Shipton

3/4 Rhythm/Bass - strum/Lively.
See Course Book No. 1 Page 22.

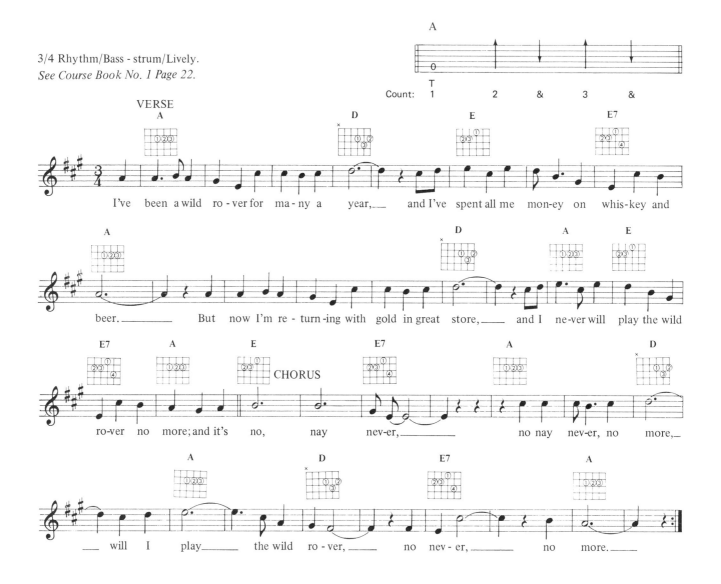

Verse 2:
I went to an alehouse I used to frequent
And I told the landlady me money was spent
I asked her for credit, she answered me "Nay"
"Such custom as yours I could have any day".

Verse 3:
I took out of me pocket ten sovereigns bright
And the landlady's eyes opened wide with delight
She said "I have whiskeys and wines of the best
And the words that you told me were only in jest."

Verse 4:
I'll go home to me parents, confess what I've done
And ask them to pardon their prodigal son
And when they've caressed me as oftimes before
I never will play the wild rover no more.

© Copyright 1982 Dorsey Bros. Music, a division of Music Sales Corporation, New York, NY
All Rights Reserved. International Copyright Secured.

Both Sides Now Joni Mitchell

4/4 Rhythm/Simple arpeggio with moving bass line.
See Course Book No. 1 Page 27.

Verse 2:
Moons and Junes, and Ferris wheels
The dizzy, dancing way you feel
As every fairy tale comes real
I've looked at love that way.
But now it's just another show
You leave 'em laughing when you go
And if you care, don't let them know
Don't give yourself away.
I've looked at love from both sides now
From give and take and still somehow
It's love's illusions I recall
I really don't know love at all.

Verse 3:
Tears and fears and feeling proud
To say "I love you" right out loud
Dreams and schemes and circus crowds
I've looked at life that way.
But now old friends are acting strange
They shake their heads, they say I've changed
But something's lost and something's gained
In living every day.
I've looked at life from both sides now
From win and lose and still somehow
It's life's illusions I recall
I really don't know life at all.

© Copyright 1967 and 1974 Siquomb Publishing Corp
All Rights Reserved. Used by permission.

Book 2

Slip Slidin' Away — Paul Simon

4/4 Rhythm/Strumming/Swing/Stress 2nd and 4th beats.
See Course Book No. 2 Page 5.

Verse 2:
I know a woman
Became a wife
These are the very words she uses to describe her life
She said "A good day ain't got no rain"
She said "A bad day is when I lie in bed"
"And think of things that might have been."

Verse 3:
And I know a father
Who had a son
He longed to tell him all the reasons for the things he'd done
He came a long way just to explain
He kissed the boy as he lay sleeping
Then he turned around and headed home again.

Verse 4:
God only knows
God makes his plan
The information is unavailable to the mortal man
We work our jobs, collect our pay
Believe we are gliding down the highway
When in fact we are slip slidin' away.

© 1977 Paul Simon. All Rights Reserved. International Copyright Secured. Used by permission.

San Francisco Bay Blues — Jesse Fuller

4/4 Rhythm/Strumming/Swing/Lively.
Book 2 Page 8.

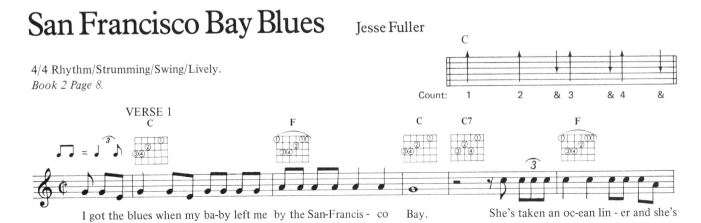

© Copyright 1958 & 1963 TRO-Hollis Music Inc., New York, NY.
All Rights Reserved. International Copyright Secured. Used by permission.

Lyin' Eyes
Don Henley and Glenn Frey

4/4 Rhythm/Strumming.
See Course Book No. 2 Page 10.

Verse 2:
Late at night a big old house gets lonely
I guess every form of refuge has its price
And it breaks her heart to think her love is only
Given to a man with hands as cold as ice.

Verse 3:
So she tells him she must go out for the evening
To comfort an old friend who's feeling down
But he know's where she's going as she's leaving
She is headed for the cheating side of town.

Verse 4:
On the other side of town a boy is waiting
With fiery eyes and dreams no-one could steal
She drives on through the night anticipating
'Cause he makes her feel the way she used to feel.

Verse 5:
She rushes to his arms, they fall together
She whispers that it's only for a while
She swears that soon she'll be coming back forever
She pulls away and leaves him with a smile.

Verse 6:
She gets up and pours herself a strong one
And stares out at the stars up in the sky
Another night, it's gonna be a long one
She draws the shade and hangs her head to cry.

Verse 7:
She wonders how it ever got this crazy
She thinks about a boy she knew in school
Did she get tired or did she just get lazy
She's so far gone she feels just like a fool.

Verse 8:
My, oh my, you sure know how to arrange things
You set it up so well, so carefully
Ain't it funny how your new life didn't change things
You're still the same old girl you used to be.

© Copyright 1975 by Benchmark Music.
All Rights Reserved. International Copyright Secured. Used by permission.

Money's The Word — Russ Shipton

4/4 Rhythm/Strumming/Stress 2nd upstroke.
See Course Book No. 2 Page 10.

Verse 2:
Now the magic man has long since gone to ground
For the music is lost in his soul and can't be found
And since the tambourine man's tambourine, up and turned to rust
The waiting list it waits, and eyes the prince's purse . . . .
But it's even money — there's a prophet's curse.

Verse 3:
There's a man from the west and he's playin' real cool guitar
And there's a guy from the east who's followin' a northern star
There's a guy underground writing longer words in lines that don't even rhyme
And the one on the inside who claims he's seen a sign . . . .
But it's even money — they've all hit the wrong time.

Verse 4:
Well the hard time traveller must be cryin' where he lays
And-a-wondrin' just what he was fighting for all his days
For the sun went down on the time when songs were sung like the call of a bird
The music man plugged in, sold out, as the businessman he stirred . . . .
And it's even money — money's the word,
Money's the word, money's the word, money's the word.

© Copyright 1982 Dorsey Bros. Music, a division of Music Sales Corporation, New York, NY
All Rights Reserved. International Copyright Secured.

Sundown — Gordon Lightfoot

Book 2

4/4 Rhythm/Strumming/Stress 2nd and 4th beats.
See Course Book No. 2 Page 10.

I can see her ly-in'-back in her sat-in dress, in a room where you do what you don't con-fess.

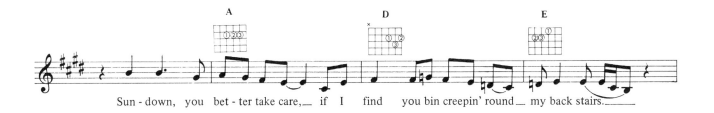

Sun-down, you bet-ter take care,— if I find you bin creepin' round— my back stairs.

Sun-down, you bet-ter take care,— if I find you bin creepin' round my back stairs.

Verse 2:
She's been lookin' like a queen in a sailor's dream
And she don't always say what she really means
Sometimes I think it's a shame
When I get feelin' better when I'm feelin' no pain
Sometimes I think it's a shame
When I get feelin' better when I'm feelin' no pain.

Verse 3:
I can picture every move that a man could make
Gettin' lost in her lovin' is your first mistake
Sundown, you better take care
If I find you bin creepin' round my back stairs
Sometimes I think it's a shame
When I get feelin' better when I'm feelin' no pain.

Verse 4:
I can see her lookin' fast in her faded jeans
She's a hard lovin' woman got me feelin' mean
Sometimes I think it's a shame
When I get feelin' better when I'm feelin' no pain
Sundown, you better take care
If I find you bin creepin' round my back stairs.

© Copyright 1973, 1974 Moose Music Ltd.
All Rights Reserved. Used by permission.

Take It Easy   Jackson Browne & Glenn Frey

4/4 Rhythm/Strumming/Stress 2nd and 4th beats.
See Course Book No. 2 Page 10.

Verse 2:
Well I'm a-standin' on a corner in Winslow, Arizona
And such a fine sight to see
It's a girl, my Lord, in a flat bed Ford
Slowin' down to take a look at me
Come on baby, don't say maybe
I gotta know if your sweet love is gonna save me
We may lose and we may win
Though we will never be here again
So open up, I'm climbin' in
So take it easy.

Verse 3:
Well I'm a-runnin' down the road tryin' to loosen my load
I gotta world of trouble on my mind
Lookin' for a lover who won't blow my cover
She's so hard to find
Take it easy, take it easy
Don't let the sound of your own wheels make you crazy
Come on baby, don't say maybe
I gotta know if your sweet love is gonna save me.

© Copyright 1972 & 1973 by Benchmark Music.
All Rights Reserved. Used by permission.

The Black Velvet Band
Traditional, arranged Russ Shipton

6/8 Rhythm/Bass-strum.
See Course Book No. 2 Page 12.

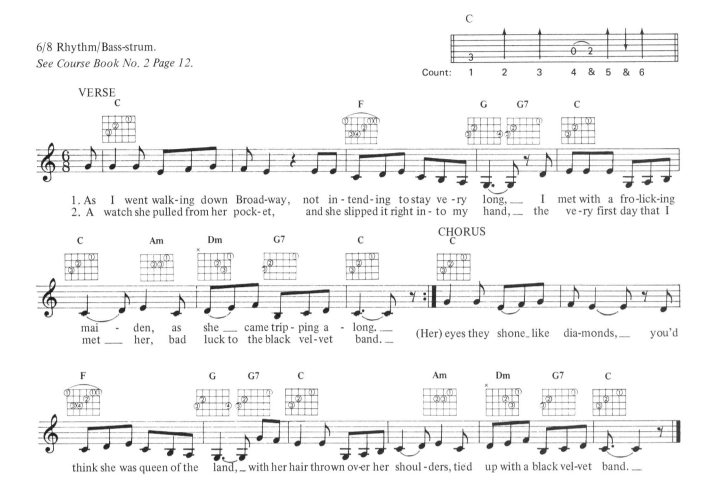

Verse 1:
1. As I went walking down Broadway, not intending to stay very long, I met with a frolicking maiden, as she came tripping along.

2. A watch she pulled from her pocket, and she slipped it right into my hand, the very first day that I met her, bad luck to the black velvet band.

CHORUS:
(Her) eyes they shone like diamonds, you'd think she was queen of the land, with her hair thrown over her shoulders, tied up with a black velvet band.

Verse 2:
'Twas in the town of Tralee
An apprenticeship to trade I was bound
With plenty of bright amusement
To see the days go round.
Till misfortune and trouble came over me
Which caused me to stray from my land
Far away from me friends and relations
To follow the black velvet band.

Verse 3:
Before the judge and the jury
The both of us had to appear
And a gentleman swore to the jewellery —
the case against us was clear.
For seven years' transportation
Right over to Van Dieman's land
Far away from me friends and relations
To follow the black velvet band.

Verse 4:
Come all you brave, young Irish lads
A warning take by me
Beware of all the pretty young damsels
That are knocking around in Tralee.
They'll treat you to whisky and porter
Until you're unable to stand
And before you have time for to leave them
You're bound for Van Dieman's land.

© Copyright 1982 Dorsey Bros. Music, a division of Music Sales Corporation, New York, NY
All Rights Reserved. International Copyright Secured.

Ridin' Blind
Russ Shipton

4/4 Rhythm/Bass - strum/Steady.
See Course Book No. 2 Page 15.

Verse 1:
With the people who aren't anywhere, watchin' all the clouds form from lighter air. The average man, like a knife, falls through here the outskirts of life.

Chorus:
Amsterdam, where are you? So far ahead, yet still behind; a thousand steps from nowhere, still looking for a sign, smile upon us lost souls ridin' blind.

Verse 2:
Seats for 50, holding 15
An American clinger and a loose-tongued singer, if you know what I mean
Roller coasters, too many toasters
A madman keeping the stage from the queen.

Verse 3:
Sufi Castenada Buddha, kindred spirits roam
Wander thru these precious grounds, saved from sea and foam
Here the searchin' wanderers come
With too much time to lose and space to run.

© Copyright 1982 Dorsey Bros. Music, a division of Music Sales Corporation, New York, NY
All Rights Reserved. International Copyright Secured.

Imagine John Lennon

Book 2

4/4 Rhythm/Arpeggio.
See Course Book No. 2 Page 20.

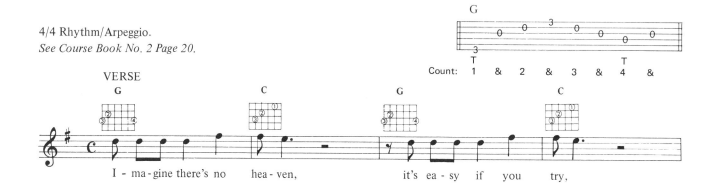

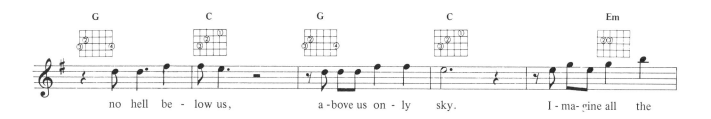

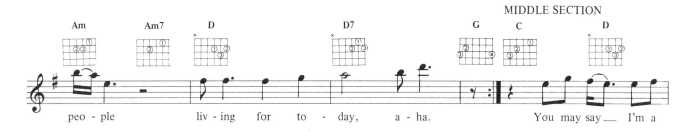

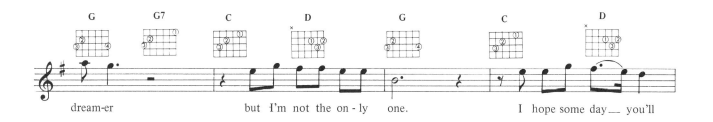

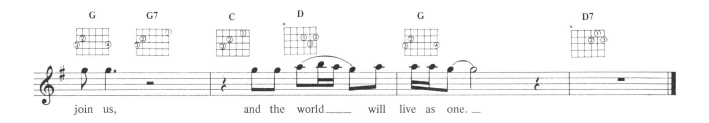

Verse 2:
Imagine there's no countries
It isn't hard to do
Nothing to kill or die for
And no religion too.
Imagine all the people
Living life in peace, aha.

Verse 3:
Imagine no possessions
I wonder if you can
No need for greed or hunger
A brotherhood of man.
Imagine all the people
Sharing all the world, aha.

Kumbaya
Traditional, arranged Russ Shipton

4/4 Rhythm/Arpeggio.
See Course Book No. 2 Page 20.

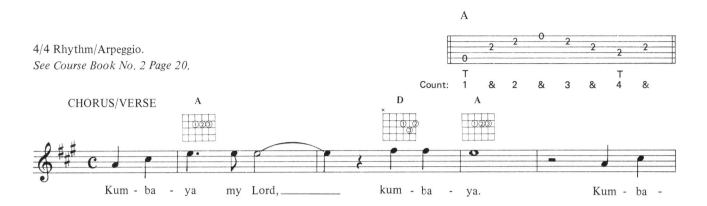

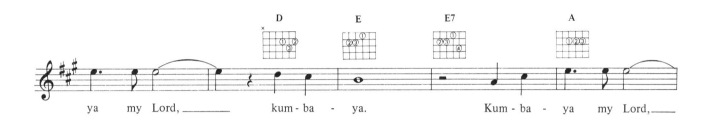

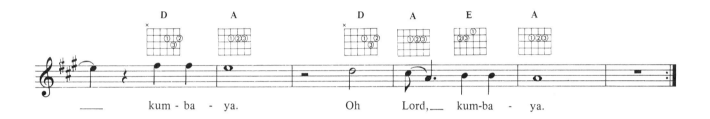

Verse 2:
Someone's crying Lord, Kumbaya
Someone's crying, Lord, Kumbaya
Someone's crying, Lord, Kumbaya
Oh Lord, Kumbaya.

Verse 3:
Someone's praying, Lord, Kumbaya
Someone's praying, Lord, Kumbaya
Someone's praying, Lord, Kumbaya
Oh Lord, Kumbaya.

Verse 4:
Someone's singing, Lord, Kumbaya
Someone's singing, Lord, Kumbaya
Someone's singing, Lord, Kumbaya
Oh Lord, Kumbaya.

© Copyright 1982 Dorsey Bros. Music, a division of Music Sales Corporation, New York, NY
All Rights Reerved. International Copyright Secured.

Book 2

April Come She Will — Paul Simon

4/4 Rhythm/Alternating thumb.
See Course Book No. 2 Page 23.

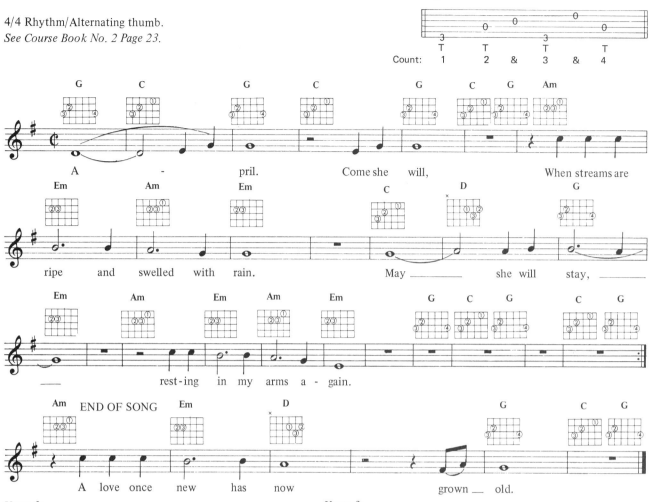

Verse 2:
June, she'll change her tune
In restless walks she'll prowl the night
July, she will fly
And give no warning to her flight.

Verse 3:
August, die she must
The autumn winds blow chilly and cold
September, I'll remember
A love once new, has now grown old.

© Copyright 1965 Paul Simon.
All Rights Reserved. International Copyright Secured. Used by permission.

Carolina In My Mind — James Taylor

4/4 Rhythm/Alternating thumb.
See Course Book No. 2 Page 23.

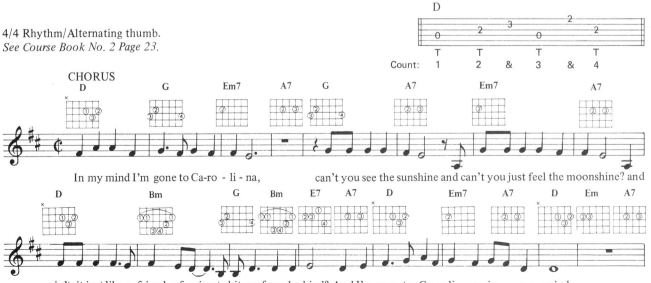

Copyright © 1969, 1970 Blackwood Music Inc. and Country Road Music Inc.
administered by Blackwood Music Inc.
All Rights Reserved. International Copyright Secured. Used by permission.

Verse 2:
Dark and silent, late last night
I think I might have heard the highway call
Geese in flight and dogs that bite
And signs that might be omens say I'm going, going
I'm gone to Carolina in my mind.

Verse 3:
There ain't no doubt in no-one's mind
That love's the finest thing around
Whisper something soft and kind
And hey, babe, the sky's on fire, I'm dying, ain't I?
I'm gone to Carolina in my mind.

The Sloop John B. Traditional, arranged Russ Shipton

4/4 Rhythm/Alternating thumb.
See Course Book No. 2 Page 23.

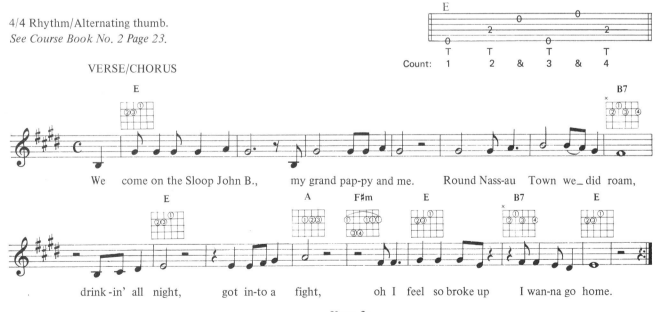

Chorus:
So hoist up the John B. sails
See how the mains'ls set
Send for the captain ashore
Let me go home, let me go home
Let me go home, I feel so broke-up
I wanna go home.

Verse 2:
The first mate, he got drunk
Broke up the people's trunk
Constable had to come and take him away
Sheriff Johnstone, please let me alone
I feel so broke-up
I wanna go home.

© Copyright 1982 Dorsey Bros. Music, a division of Music Sales Corporation, New York, NY
All Rights Reserved. International Copyright Secured.

Only Hopes Returning — Russ Shipton

Book 2

4/4 Rhythm/Alternating thumb.
See Course Book No. 2 Page 25.

There were times I know we were sad, I can't de-ny those hard times we had, but some-times you and I could near-ly hit the sky, and I'd take it all a-gain both good and bad. And I thought I heard your voice a call-ing, say-ing words that were soft and kind, but it was on-ly my hopes re-turn-ing, ech-o-ing a-round this emp-ty world of mine.

Verse 2:
I'm like a flower trying to bloom in Winter snows
I'm like the North wind wondrin' where to blow
I see your smiling face,
I miss every line and trace
And in my dreams you call me sweet and low.

Verse 3:
I'm trapped just like the convict in his cell
Goin' over and over those things I knew so well
I'd love to hear the sound
Of your footsteps on the ground
You know I'd reach the door before you touched the bell.

© Copyright 1982 Dorsey Bros. Music, a division of Music Sales Corporation, New York, NY
All Rights Reserved. International Copyright Secured.

Help John Lennon and Paul McCartney

4/4 Rhythm/Strumming/Fast.
See Course Book No. 3 Page 6.

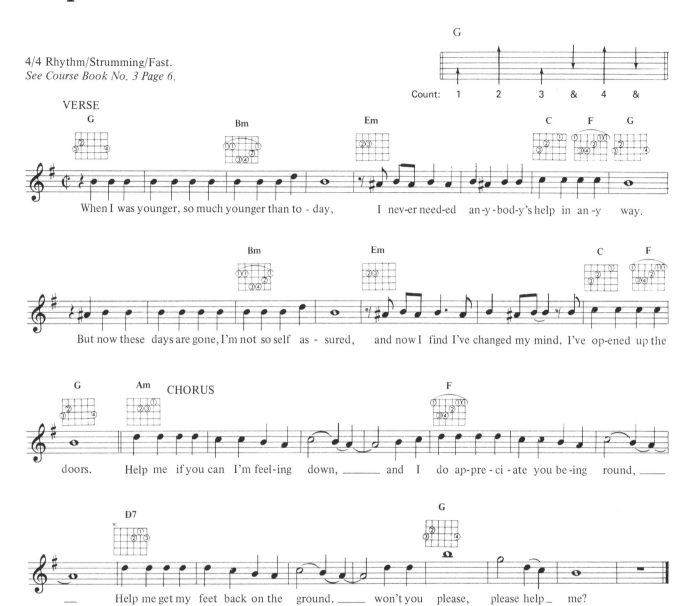

Verse 2:
And now my life has changed in oh so many ways.
My independence seems to vanish in the haze.
But every now and then I feel so insecure
I know that I just need you like I've never done before.

© Copyright 1965 Northern Songs Limited, London, England.
All rights for the United States of America, Mexico and the Philippines controlled by
MACLEN MUSIC INC. c/o ATV Music Corp., 6255 Sunset Blvd., Los Angeles, CA 90028.
All Rights Reserved. International Copyright Secured. Used by permission.

Frankie And Johnny
Traditional, arranged Russ Shipton

4/4 Rhythm/Bass-strum/Swing.
See Course Book No. 3 Page 11.

Frankie and Johnny were lovers, ___ oh lordy how they could love. They swore to be true to each other true as the stars above. He was her man, but he was doing her wrong.

Verse 2:
Frankie, she was a good woman
As everybody knows
Spent a hundred dollars
Just to buy her man some clothes
He was her man, but he was doing her wrong.

Verse 3:
Frankie went down to the corner
Just for a bucket of beer
She said "Oh Mister bartender"
"Has my loving Johnny been here?"
He was her man, but he was doing her wrong.

Verse 4:
"Now I don't wanna tell you no stories
And I don't wanna tell you no lies
I saw Johnny 'bout an hour ago
With a gal named Nelly Bligh."
He was her man, but he was doing her wrong.

Verse 5:
Now Frankie went down to the hotel
Didn't go there for fun
Underneath her long dress
She carried a forty-four gun
He was her man, but he was doing her wrong.

Verse 6:
Well the first time that Frankie shot Johnny
He let out an awful yell
Second time that she shot him
There was a new man's face in hell.
He was her man, but he was doing her wrong.

© Copyright 1982 Dorsey Bros. Music, a division of Music Sales Corporation, New York, NY
All Rights Reserved. International Copyright Secured.

Worried Man Blues
Traditional, arranged Russ Shipton

4/4 Rhythm/Bass - strum/Slight swing.
See Course Book No. 3 Page 11.

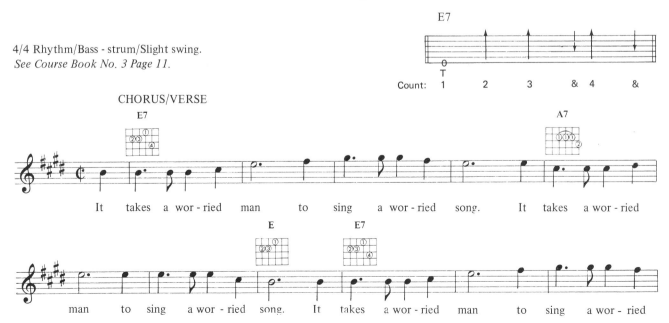

CHORUS/VERSE

It takes a worried man to sing a worried song. It takes a worried man to sing a worried song. It takes a worried man to sing a worried

© Copyright 1982 Dorsey Bros. Music, a division of Music Sales Corporation, New York, NY
All Rights Reserved. International Copyright Secured.

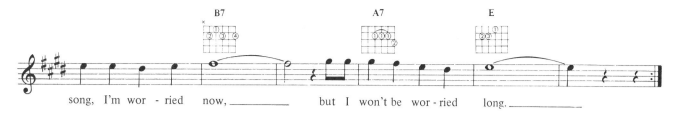

song, I'm wor - ried now, but I won't be wor - ried long.

Verse 2:
I went across the river, and I lay down to sleep
I went across the river, and I lay down to sleep
I went across the river, and I lay down to sleep
When I woke up, I had shackles on my feet.

Verse 3:
When everything goes wrong, I sing a worried song
When everything goes wrong, I sing a worried song
When everything goes wrong, I sing a worried song
I'm worried now, but I won't be worried long.

All My Trials Traditional, arranged Russ Shipton

4/4 Rhythm/Syncopated arpeggio.
See Course Book No. 3 Page 16.

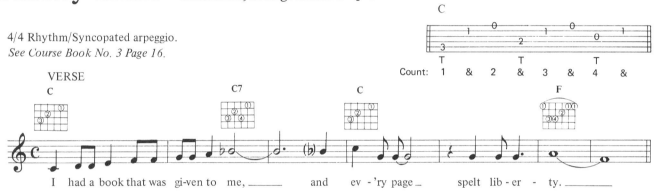

I had a book that was gi-ven to me, and ev-'ry page spelt lib - er - ty.

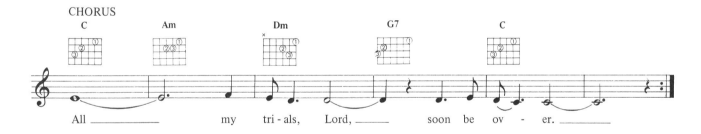

All my tri - als, Lord, soon be ov - er.

Too late my bro - thers, too late, but nev - er mind.

Verse 2:
If religion were a thing that money could buy
The rich would live, and the poor would die.

Verse 3:
There is a tree in paradise
The pilgrims call it the tree of life.

Verse 4:
Jordan water is chilly and cold
Chills the body, but not the soul.

Verse 5:
Hush little baby, don't you cry
Your momma was born to die.

Diamonds And Rust — Joan Baez

4/4 Rhythm/Syncopated arpeggio.
See Course Book No. 3 Page 16.

Lyrics under music:
1. Well, I'll be damned, here comes your ghost a-gain, but that's not un-us-u-al, it's just that the moon is full, and you happ-ened to call.
2. And here I sit, hand on the tel-e-phone, I'm hear-ing a voice I'd known a cou-ple of light years ago, head-ing straight for a fall.

MIDDLE SECTION: Now I see you stand-ing with brown leaves fall-ing all a-round and snow in your hair. Now you're smil-ing out the win-dow of that crum-my ho-tel ov-er Wash-ing-ton Square. Our breath comes out white clouds, mingles and hangs in the air. Speak-ing strict-ly for me, we both could have died then and there.

Verse 2:
As I remember
Your eyes were bluer than robins' eggs
My poetry was lousy, you said
Where are you calling from?
A booth in mid-west.
Ten years ago
I bought you some cufflinks
You bought me something
We both know what memories can bring
They bring diamonds and rust.

Verse 3:
You burst on the scene
Already a legend
The unwashed phenomenon
The original vagabond
You strayed into my arms.
And there you stayed
Temporarily lost at sea
The madonna was yours for free
Yes the girl on the half shell
Could keep you unharmed.

Verse 4:
Now you're telling me you're not nostalgic
Then give me another word for it
You who're so good with words
And at keeping things vague.
'Cause I need some of that vagueness now
It's all come back too clearly
Yes I loved you dearly
And if you're offering me diamonds and rust
I've already paid.

© Copyright 1975 Chandos Music (ASCAP).
All Rights Reserved. International Copyright Secured. Used by permission.

Your Song
Elton John & Bernie Taupin

4/4 Rhythm/Syncopated arpeggio with pinches.
See Course Book No. 3 Page 16.

Verse 2:
If I was a sculptor, but then again, no
Or a man who makes potions in a travelling show
I know it's not much but, it's the best I can do
My gift is my song, and this one's for you.

Verse 3:
I sat on the roof, and kicked off the moss
Well a few of the verses, they got me quite cross
But the sun's been quite kind while I wrote this song
It's for people like you that keep me turned on.

Verse 4:
So excuse me forgetting, but these things I do
You see I've forgotten if they're green or they're blue
Anyway, the thing is, what I really mean
Yours are the sweetest eyes I've ever seen.

Copyright © 1969 Dick James Music Limited, London, England.
All rights for the United States of America and Canada controlled by
Dick James Music, Inc. 24 Music Square East, Nashville, TN 37203.
International Copyright Secured. All Rights Reserved

Mr Bojangles — Jerry Jeff Walker

3/4 Rhythm/Arpeggio/Swing.
See Course Book No. 3 Page 17.

Verse 2:
I met him in a cell in New Orleans I was, down and out
He looked at me to be the eyes of age, as he spoke right out
He talked of life, talked of life
He laughed, slapped his leg a step.

Verse 3:
He said his name, Bojangles, then he danced a lick across the cell
He grabbed his pants for a better stance then he jumped so high
He clicked his heels
Then he let go a laugh, let go a laugh
Shook back his clothes all around.

Verse 4:
He danced for those at minstrel shows and county fairs
Throughout the South
He spoke with tears of fifteen years how his dog and him
Travelled about
His dog up and died, he up and died
And after twenty years he still grieved.

Verse 5:
He said "I dance now at every chance in honky tonks
For drinks and tips
But most the time I spend behind these county bars
For I drinks a bit."
He shook his head, and as he shook his head
I heard someone ask "Please".

© Copyright 1968 by Cotillion Music Inc. & Danel Music Inc.
All Rights Reserved. International Copyright Secured.

I'll Have To Say I Love You In A Song — Jim Croce

4/4 Rhythm/Syncopated arpeggio.
See Course Book No. 3 Page 20.

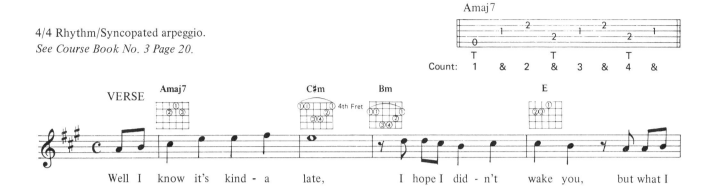

VERSE: Well I know it's kind-a late, I hope I did-n't wake you, but what I

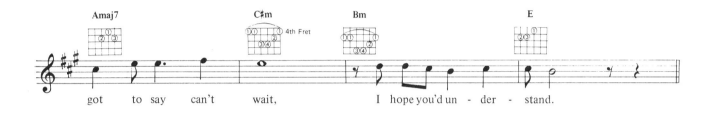

got to say can't wait, I hope you'd un-der-stand.

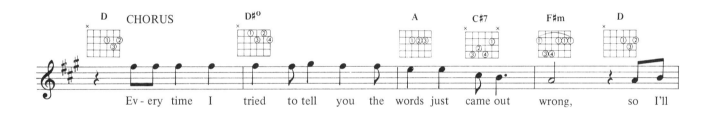

CHORUS: Ev-ery time I tried to tell you the words just came out wrong, so I'll

have to say I love you in a song.

Verse 2:
Yeah I know it's kinda strange
But every time I'm near you
I just run out of things to say
I know you'd understand.

Verse 3:
Yeah I know it's kinda late
I hope I didn't wake you
But there's something that I just got to say
I know you'd understand.

Copyright © 1971, 1972 BLENDINGWELL MUSIC, INC.
Copyright © 1971, 1972 in U.S.A. and Canada BLENDINGWELL MUSIC, INC. and MCA MUSIC, a division of MCA Inc.
All Rights Reserved. Used by permission.

Plumstones — Russ Shipton

Book 3

4/4 Rhythm/Syncopated arpeggio.
See Course Book No. 3 Page 20.

VERSE
A child of the twen-ties, that was my fath-er's time and all the dreams he might have had were fruit left up-on the vine and ne-ver picked. He learnt a trick or two, the cavalry it saw him through. But that was a-no-ther day, when

CHORUS
nose to the grind-stone was the on-ly way. Tin-ker, tai-lor, sol-dier, sail-or, which one will you be? Rich man, poor man, beggar man, thief,— lit-tle boy on my knee, don't let your dreams go free.

ENDING
see, but don't let your dreams go free.

Verse 2:
A child of the fifties
Born with a new age dawning
I had bigger brighter better dreams
But in my head was my father's warning
Son, you've got to play the game
Work is still a sacred name
But that was another day
When freedom was just a word
We'd learnt to say.

Verse 3:
A child of the eighties
Here on my knee you sit
Counting all your plumstones
Just the way I did
When I was young
And you have your dreams too
All the things you'd like to do
It's not just another day
You can live your dreams
Don't throw 'em away.

Last Chorus:
Tinker, tailor, soldier, sailor
Which one will you be?
Rich man, poor man, beggarman, thief?
Little boy on my knee
Count your plumstones and see
But don't let your dreams go free.

© Copyright 1982 Dorsey Bros. Music, a division of Music Sales Corporation, New York, NY
All Rights Reserved. International Copyright Secured.

There But For Fortune — Phil Ochs

4/4 Rhythm/Syncopated arpeggio.
See Course Book No. 3 Page 20.

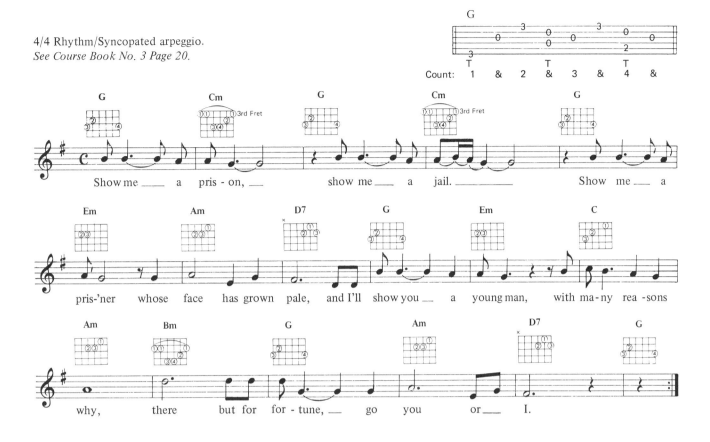

Show me a pris-on, show me a jail. Show me a pris-'ner whose face has grown pale, and I'll show you a young man, with ma-ny rea-sons why, there but for for-tune, go you or I.

Verse 2:
Show me an alley, show me a train
Show me a hobo who sleeps out in the rain
And I'll show you a young man with many reasons why
There but for fortune, go you or I.

Verse 3:
Show me the whiskey stains on the floor
Show me a drunk as he stumbles out the door
And I'll show you a young man with many reasons why
There but for fortune, go you or I.

Verse 4:
Show me a country where the bombs had to fall
Show me the ruins of buildings so tall
And I'll show you a young land with many reasons why
There but for fortune, go you or I.

© Copyright 1963 Appleseed Music Inc.
All Rights Reserved. International Copyright Secured.

Book 3

The Boxer — Paul Simon

4/4 Rhythm/Alternating thumb.
See Course Book No. 3 Page 23.

VERSE

I am just a poor boy, though my stor-y's sel-dom told, I have squand-ered my re-sis-tance for a pock-et-ful of mum-bles, such are pro-mi-ses. All lies and jest, still a man hears what he wants to hear, and dis-re-gards the rest, ooh la la, la la la la la la la.

CHORUS

Lie la lie, lie la lie la lie la lie, lie la lie, lie la lie la la la lie la la la lie.

End of 4th verse

lead-ing me _____ go-ing home. _____

Verse 2:
When I left my home and my family, I was no more than a boy
In the company of strangers, in the quiet of a railway station
Running scared, laying low, seeking out the poorer quarters
Where the ragged people go, looking for the places only they would know.

Verse 3:
Asking only workman's wages, I come looking for a job
But I get no offers, just a come-on from the whores on 7th Avenue
I do declare, there were times when I was so lonesome
I took some comfort there.

Verse 4:
Then I'm laying out my winter clothes and wishing I was gone
Going home, where the New York City winters aren't bleeding me
Leading me, going home.

Verse 5:
In the clearing stands a boxer, and a fighter by his trade
And he carries the reminders of every glove that laid him down
Or cut him till he cried out in his anger and his shame
"I am leaving, I am leaving," but the fighter still remains.

© 1968 Paul Simon. All Rights Reserved. International Copyright Secured. Used by permission.

Early Mornin' Rain — Gordon Lightfoot

4/4 Rhythm/Alternating thumb.
See Course Book No. 3 Page 23.

Verse 2:

Out on runway number nine
Big seven-o-seven set to go
But I'm stuck here in the grass
Where the cold wind blows
Now the liquor tasted good
And the women all were fast
Well there she goes, my friend
She's rollin' now at last.

Verse 3:

Hear the mighty engines roar
See the silver bird on high
She's away and westward bound
Far above the clouds she'll fly
Where the mornin' rain don't fall
And the sun always shines
She'll be flyin' o'er my home
In about three hours time.

Verse 4:

This old airport's got me down
It's no earthly good to me
'Cause I'm stuck here on the ground
As cold and drunk as I can be
You can't jump a jet plane
Like you can a freight train
So I'd best be on my way
In the early mornin' rain.

© Copyright 1964 & 1966 by Warner Bros. Publications, Inc.
All Rights Reserved. Used by permission.

Fire And Rain — James Taylor

4/4 Rhythm/Arpeggio & alternating thumb mix.
See Course Book No. 3 Page 25.

Verse 2:
Look down upon me Jesus, you gotta help me make a stand
You've just gotta see me through another day
My body's aching, and my time is at hand
And I won't make it any other way.

Verse 3:
Walking my mind to an easy time, my back turned towards the sun
Lord knows when the cold wind blows, it'll turn your head around
Well, those hours of time on the telephone line
To talk about things to come
Sweet dreams and flyin' machines in pieces on the ground.

Copyright © 1969, 1970 Blackwood Music Inc. and Country Road Music Inc.
administered by Blackwood Music Inc.
All Rights Reserved. International Copyright Secured. Used by permission.

Something George Harrison

4/4 Rhythm/Ballad strum.
See Course Book No. 4 Page 7.

Verse 2:
Somewhere in her smile, she knows
That I don't need no other lover
Something in her style that shows me
I don't want to leave her now
You know I believe and how.

Verse 3:
Something in the way she knows
And all I have to do is think of her
Something in the things she shows me
I don't want to leave her now
You know I believe and how.

© Copyright 1969 Harrisongs Limited.
All Rights Reserved. International Copyright Secured.

Just The Way You Are — Billy Joel

Book 4

4/4 Rhythm/Strumming/Stress 1st beat and 1st upstroke slightly.
See Course Book No. 4 Page 10.

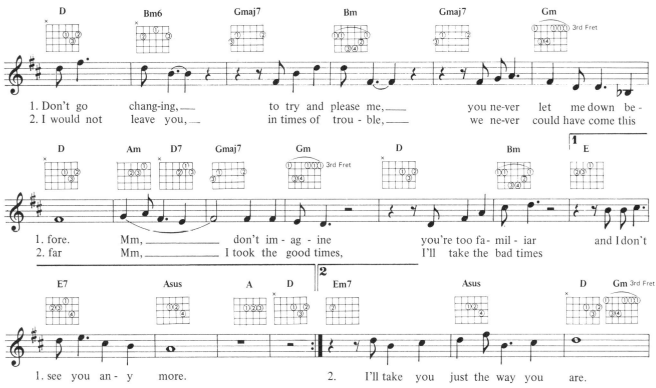

1. Don't go chang-ing, to try and please me, you ne-ver let me down be-fore. Mm, don't im-ag-ine you're too fa-mil-iar and I don't see you an-y more.
2. I would not leave you, in times of trou-ble, we ne-ver could have come this far. Mm, I took the good times, I'll take the bad times. 2. I'll take you just the way you are.

MIDDLE SECTION

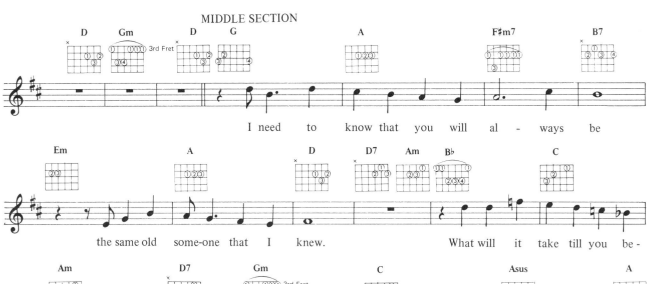

I need to know that you will al-ways be the same old some-one that I knew. What will it take till you be-

-lieve in me, the way that I be-lieve in you?

Verse 2:
Don't go trying some new fashion
Don't change the colour of your hair mm mm
You always have my unspoken passion
Although I might not seem to care.
I don't want clever conversation
I never want to work that hard, mm mm
I just want someone that I can talk to
I want you just the way you are.

Verse 3:
I said I love you, and that's forever
And this I promise from the heart, mm mm
I could not love you any better
I love you just the way you are.

Copyright © 1977 Impulsive Music and April Music Inc.
administered by April Music Inc.
All Rights Reserved. International Copyright Secured. Used by permission.

May You Never — John Martyn

4/4 Rhythm/Slap style.
See Course Book No. 4 Page 11.

Verse 2:
May you never lose your temper
If you get in a barroom fight
May you never lose your woman overnight.
You've been just like a good and close brother of mine
And you know I love you like I should.
You've got no knife to stab me in the back
And I know that there's those that would.

© Copyright 1973 & 1978 Warlock Music Ltd.
Controlled in the U.S.A. and Canada by ACKEE MUSIC INC.
All Rights Reserved. Used by permission.

Sunny Afternoon
Raymond Douglas Davies

Book 4

4/4 Rhythm/Strumming/Swing/Damp downstrokes.
See Course Book No. 4 Page 11.

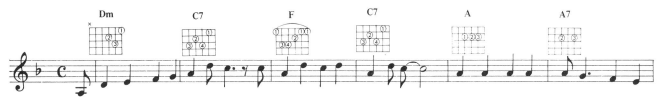

The tax-man's tak-en all my dough, and left me in my state-ly home, laz-ing on a sun-ny aft-er-

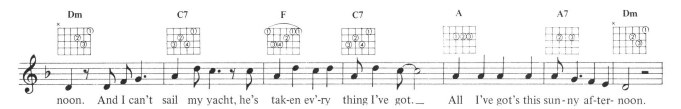

noon. And I can't sail my yacht, he's tak-en ev'-ry thing I've got. All I've got's this sun-ny af-ter- noon.

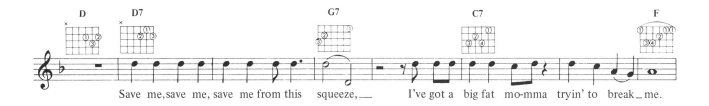

Save me, save me, save me from this squeeze, I've got a big fat mo-mma tryin' to break me.

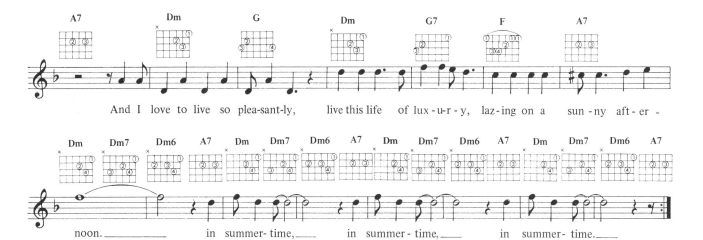

And I love to live so plea-sant-ly, live this life of lux-u-r-y, laz-ing on a sun-ny aft-er- noon. in summer- time, in summer - time, in summer- time.

Verse 2:
My girlfriend's gone off with my car
And gone back to her ma and pa
Telling tales of drunkenness and cruelty
Now I'm sitting here
Sipping at my ice-cold beer
Lazing on a sunny afternoon.
Help me, help me, help me sail away
You give me two good reasons
Why I ought to stay.
'Cause I love to live so pleasantly
Live this life of luxury
Lazing on a sunny afternoon
In summertime, in summertime, in summertime.

Copyright © 1966 by Belinda (London) Ltd.
Controlled in the U.S.A. by Unichappell Music, Inc. (Rightsong Music, publisher) and
Abkco Music, Inc.
International Copyright Secured. All Rights Reserved.
Unauthorized copying, arranging, adapting, recording or public performance is an
infringement of copyright.

Here Comes The Sun   George Harrison

4/4 Rhythm/Alternating thumb.
See Course Book No. 4 Page 14.

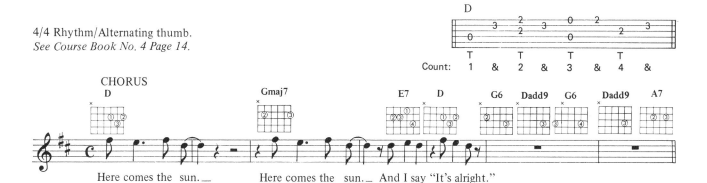

CHORUS

Here comes the sun. Here comes the sun. And I say "It's alright."

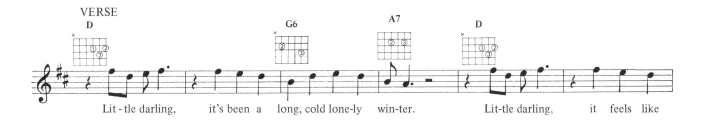

VERSE

Lit-tle darling, it's been a long, cold lone-ly win-ter. Lit-tle darling, it feels like

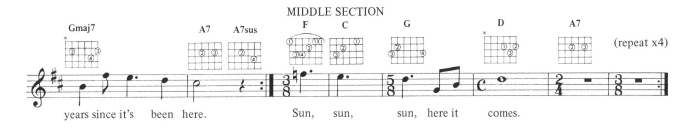

MIDDLE SECTION

years since it's been here. Sun, sun, sun, here it comes. (repeat x4)

TAG (after last repeat of middle section)

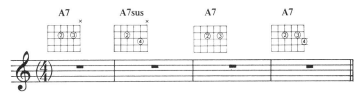

Verse 2:

Little darling, the smiles returning to their faces
Little darling, it seems like years since it's been here.

Verse 3:

Little darling, I feel that ice is slowly melting
Little darling, it seems like years since it's been clear.

© Copyright 1969 Harrisongs Limited.
All Rights Reserved. International Copyright Secured.

Skyline Russ Shipton

3/4 Rhythm/Arpeggio and embellishments.
See Course Book No. 4 pages 16-22.

♦ = harmonic (always at 12th fret)

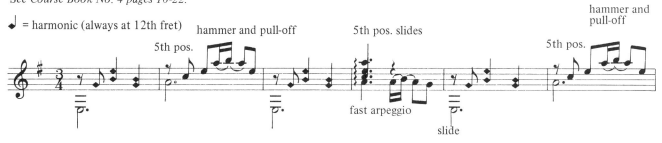

© Copyright 1982 Dorsey Bros. Music, a division of Music Sales Corporation, New York, NY
All Rights Reserved. International Copyright Secured.

Snowmobiling Russ Shipton

4/4 Rhythm/Alternating thumb in D tuning with embellishments.
See Course Book No. 4 Pages 16-22.

1st D
2nd A
3rd F# } 'D' Tuning
4th D
5th A
6th D

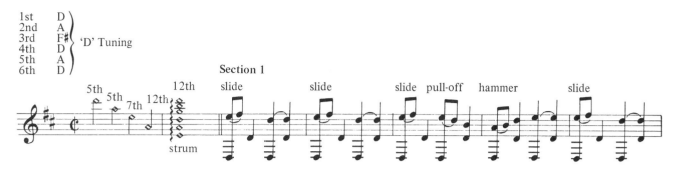

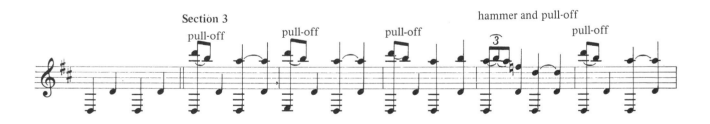

© Copyright 1982 Dorsey Bros. Music, a division of Music Sales Corporation, New York, NY
All Rights Reserved. International Copyright Secured.

Book 4

The Third Waltz — Russ Shipton

3/8 Rhythm/Arpeggio and embellishments with 3rds.
See Course Book No. 4 Pages 16-22 & 26.

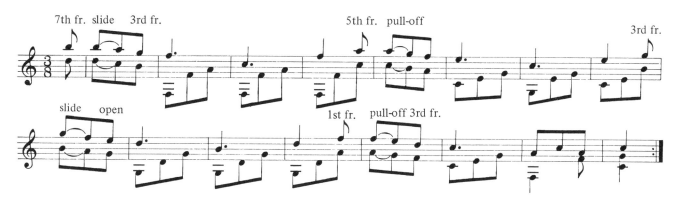

© Copyright 1982 Dorsey Bros. Music, a division of Music Sales Corporation, New York, NY
All Rights Reserved. International Copyright Secured.

G. Wizz — Russ Shipton

4/4 Rhythm/Syncopated arpeggio and alternating thumb mix. (Right hand thumb plays 1st & 2nd bass string notes in each bar, one after the other).
See Course Book No. 4 Page 23.

© Copyright 1982 Dorsey Bros. Music, a division of Music Sales Corporation, New York, NY
All Rights Reserved. International Copyright Secured.

You've Got A Friend   Carole King

4/4 Rhythm/Syncopated arpeggio and alternating thumb mix.
See Course Book No. 4 Page 23.

Verse 2:
If the sky, above you, should turn dark and full of clouds
And that old north wind should begin to blow
Keep your head together, and call my name out loud
And soon, you'll hear me knocking upon your door.

Copyright © 1971 by Screen Gems-EMI Music and Colgems-EMI Music, Inc.
All Rights Reserved. Used by permission.

Book 4

Classical Capers   Russ Shipton

6/8 Rhythm/Triplets and pinches.
See Course Book No. 4 Page 29.

Section 1

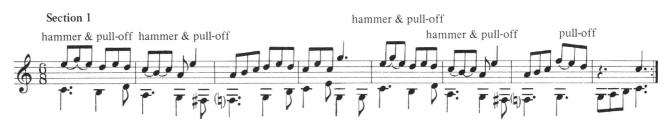

Section 2

Section 3

© Copyright 1982 Dorsey Bros. Music, a division of Music Sales Corporation, New York, NY
All Rights Reserved. International Copyright Secured.